Silly Shakespeare for Students

I0517957

TWELFTH NIGHT

PAUL LEONARD MURRAY

with help from

WILLIAM SHAKESPEARE

Alphabet PUBLISHING

ISBN: 978-1-956159-53-0 (paperback)
ISBN: 978-1-956159-54-7 (ebook)

For permission requests or discounts on class sets and bulk orders contact us at:

Alphabet Publishing
29 Milo Drive
Branford, CT 06405 USA

info@alphabetpublishingbooks.com
www.alphabetpublishingbooks.com

For performance rights, please contact Paul Murray at paulplaying@gmail.com

Interior Formatting and Cover Design by Melissa Williams Design

Za moju Milicu

The Story Behind Shakespeare's Twelfth Night

Twelfth Night, otherwise known as *What You Will*, was written by William Shakespeare in the early 1600s. It is a comedic tale of love, mistaken identities, and playful mischief. Set in the land of Illyria (now Croatia), it follows Viola, who disguises herself as a man, leading to a tangle of romantic pursuits. Themes of love, gender, and social class resonate, making it a timeless exploration of youthful passion and confusion, appealing to teenagers navigating their own relationships.

The History of Twelfth Night

The first recorded performance of the place was on the 2nd of February 1602 in London.

The title refers to the Twelfth Night of the Christmas season, a time of revelry and role reversal, reflecting the play's themes of chaos and celebration. Shakespeare often drew inspiration from folklore and classical stories, blending them into rich narratives.

The Plot of Twelfth Night

The story begins with Viola, who is shipwrecked in the fictional land of Illyria. Believing her twin brother, Sebastian, has drowned, she disguises herself as a boy named Cesario to find work. She ends up serving Duke Orsino, who is in love with the beautiful Countess Olivia.

Olivia, however, is mourning her brother and has sworn off love. But when Cesario (Viola) comes to woo her on Orsino's behalf, Olivia falls for Cesario instead, not knowing he's actually a woman.

Meanwhile, Sir Toby Belch, Olivia's uncle, and his friends play pranks on Malvolio, Olivia's uptight steward, who has ambitions of marrying her. Their schemes lead to hilarious misunderstandings and chaos.

Eventually, Sebastian shows up, causing even more confusion as everyone mistakes him for Cesario. The play wraps up with multiple weddings and the revelation of true identities, emphasizing that love can be unpredictable and sometimes a little crazy.

Major Characters

1. **Viola**: The play's protagonist who disguises herself as Cesario. Her intelligence, resourcefulness, and emotional depth drive much of the plot.

2. **Duke Orsino**: The lovesick duke who pines for Olivia. He represents the theme of romantic idealism, often oblivious to the feelings of those around him.

3. **Olivia**: A wealthy countess mourning her brother's death. Her rejection of Orsino's advances sets off a chain of events that ultimately leads to her unexpected romance with Sebastian.

4. **Malvolio**: Olivia's steward whose ambition and self-righteousness make him a target for ridicule. His subplot offers a critical look at social ambition and pretentiousness.

5. **Sir Toby Belch**: Olivia's uncle, a reveller who embodies the spirit of festivity. He represents the carefree attitude of the lower gentry.

6. **Sir Andrew Aguecheek**: A foolish suitor to Olivia,

he provides comic relief and highlights the theme of misguided ambition.

7. **Clown:** The fool, who offers wisdom and insight beneath his playful exterior. He serves as a commentator on the action and themes of the play.

8. **Sebastian:** Viola's twin brother, whose arrival complicates the love dynamics and ultimately resolves many of the misunderstandings.

Themes

1. **Love and Desire:** The play examines different kinds of love—romantic, platonic, and unrequited. The confusion and complexity of love are central, particularly with Viola's disguise complicating her feelings for Duke Orsino.

2. **Identity and Disguise:** Viola's cross-dressing as Cesario raises questions about gender identity and the nature of self. The play challenges societal norms and expectations regarding gender roles.

3. **Folly and Misunderstanding:** Many characters fall victim to misunderstandings and deception, leading to humorous situations. The folly of characters like Malvolio highlights the theme of social ambition and the foolishness of pride.

4. **Festivity and Celebration:** The setting during the Christmas season underscores themes of revelry, transformation, and the breaking of social norms.

5. **Social Class and Ambition:** Characters like Malvolio desire upward mobility, leading to comedic yet critical commentary on class distinctions and aspirations.

Playing Style

This version of *Twelfth Night*, although reduced to around a one-hour playing time, remains true to the original's plot, characters (with some small exceptions), and structure. When performed, this production should maintain a lively pace and exaggerated style. Technically, the production, as with the original, has a low level of technical requirements. The sets can be very minimal and the costumes simple. A musical score may be useful between scenes to cover changes where necessary and it would be natural that the character of the Clown is the musician.

Of course, one of the major differences between this version and the original is the simplification of the text. On some occasions, in performance, you will find the rhyming scheme helpful to the playing, in which case the actors should just 'stand back,' enjoy the words and help the audience do the same. On other occasions, the rhyming scheme will seem stifling and restrictive, in which case, do not be afraid to improvise a little, add your own occasional lines, or do not emphasise the rhymes so much. Overall, this version should be fun to play and watch. It can be produced with a small budget and should be performed in an 'over the top' manner which can give you a chance to play with your own ideas of theatricality.

Cast of Characters

ORSINO, *Duke of Illyria*
SEBASTIAN, *brother to Viola*
ANTONIA, *a sea captain, friend to Sebastian*
A SEA CAPTAIN, *friend to Viola*
VALENTINE, *gentleman attending on the Duke*
CURIO, *A gentleman attending the Duke*
SIR TOBY BELCH, *uncle to Olivia*
SIR ANDREW AGUECHEEK
MALVOLIO, *steward to Olivia*
FABIAN, *servant to Olivia*
FESTE, *a clown, servant to Olivia*
OLIVIA
VIOLA
MARIA, *Olivia's woman*

*Lords, priests, sailors, officers, musicians,
and other attendants*

Act I

Scene I

Duke Orsino's palace

['The Wild Rover' music is playing as DUKE ORSINO and CURIO are waiting outside the gate of a fancy house.]

CLOWN

[As narrator, singing to the tune of 'The Wild Rover']

Twelfth Night is a famous Shakespearean play!
So lend me your ears, and we'll get underway!
It's a story of yearning, of love, and disguise,
Of ambition, and gender deceiving your eyes
It's the best play ever. *[clap, clap, clap, clap]*
But I'll sing now no more.
We will join our first lovebird
As he waits at a door!

DUKE ORSINO
[Aside] I love the fair Olivia
And all my love I give to her.
But she will not reciprocate.
That's why I'm waiting at her gate.
I sent my servant, Valentine,
To ask the lady to be mine.
Without her love, I'll surely die.
I'm hoping for a swift reply!

[Enter VALENTINE from the house]

VALENTINE
My noble lord, Duke Orsino,
The lady wanted you to know
That, having lost her little brother
She definitely can't take a lover.
Her voice it shivers, her eyes have tears.
She said, 'Come back in seven years!'

[Exit VALENTINE into the house]

DUKE ORSINO
[Aside] How strong that woman's love must be
To keep herself away from me.
Of course the lady she must grieve.
But seven years! I can't believe
That she can resist me for that long.
If music's the food for love, play on!

[Romantic music]

Until that lady's heart I've won.
I don't give up so easily.
I'll come back when I have plan B.

SCENE II.

The seacoast

[VIOLA and a Sea Captain lying on a beach]

CAPTAIN
No soul than mine is wearier.
We've landed in Illyria.

VIOLA
Well more like crashed than landed.

CAPTAIN
My ship was wrecked . . .

VIOLA
　　　　and we are stranded.

CAPTAIN
But stranded on a lovely isle.
I suggest that we should stay a while.

VIOLA
We are very lucky to be alive.
My brother Sebastian did not survive!

CAPTAIN
He may be in the neighbourhood.
I saw him drifting on some wood.
With a friendly wind and helpful tide,
He may yet join you by your side.

VIOLA
Your words, dear Captain, ease my fear.
Do you know Illyria?

CAPTAIN
Duke Orsino does rule this place.
He loves Olivia, but she hides her face.
She still does mourn her brother's dispatch
And is not in the mood for a romantic match.

VIOLA
I understand the sister's pain
But she should learn to love again.
[Decisively standing] In Orsino's court, I'll play my part
And help him win Olivia's heart.
I'll help the lord the lady to woo.
I've now got nothing better to do!

[Beginning to disguise herself]

But as these men they don't hire girls,
I'll tie up all my ladies' curls.
I'll play a man with the pronoun 'he'.
Cesario I'll pretend to be!

CAPTAIN
This plan will help you much recover
From losing Seb, your dearest brother.

VIOLA
Now help me with my keen disguise
That I may fool Illyrian eyes!

CENE III.

OLIVIA'S house

[Enter drunk SIR TOBY BELCH and MARIA]

MARIA
Sir Toby please try not to shout.
Olivia's light has just gone out.

SIR TOBY BELCH
Maria! Is that a final warning?

MARIA
Your niece, my Lord, she is in mourning.

SIR TOBY BELCH
I tried mourning once but I ended up thinking
It just gets in the way of drinking!

MARIA
Your drinking pal who came last week . . .

SIR TOBY BELCH
You mean Sir Andrew Aguecheek?
[Referring to his height] He's *longing* for Olivia.

MARIA
That fact is nought but trivia.
She *longs* for men to leave her be!

SIR TOBY BELCH
Talk of the devil, here is he!

[Enter SIR ANDREW]

SIR ANDREW
Sir Toby Belch, you sly old rake!

MARIE
Oh please be calm, for goodness's sake!

SIR ANDREW
Oh that I could keep my calm,
When I see Olivia's charm!

MARIA
With my mistress you have no chance!

SIR ANDREW
Just wait until she sees me dance!

SIR TOBY BELCH
He kicks a caper, skips a jig.

[SIR ANDREW dances wildly and stumbles.]

MARIA
You fall again you'll lose your wig!

SIR ANDREW
I'll have you know this hair's all mine.

SIR TOBY BELCH
Bought and paid for, from a swine!

MARIA
Now listen, boys, be good and sleep.

[Maria EXITS]

SIR TOBY BELCH
Those who are deaf won't hear a peep!

SIR ANDREW
I will not stay a second more.
Your niece she hates me, that's for sure!

SIR TOBY BELCH
You should stay and take your chances.
You know she spurns the dukes' advances.
She doesn't go for brains or style!

SIR ANDREW
Then maybe I *will* stay a while!

SCENE IV.

Duke Orsino's palace

[Enter VALENTINE with VIOLA in man's clothing]

VIOLA
[Aside] Three days I've been in the duke's employ,
And he thinks of me only as a boy.

[To VALENTINE]

Duke Orsino has lovely eyes.
He's serious, kind, witty, and wise.

VALENTINE
You sound like you do fancy him!

VIOLA
Oh no, no, no, I like wo-men.

[Enter DUKE ORSINO]

DUKE ORSINO
Cesario, now where is he?

VIOLA
I'm here, my lord.

DUKE ORSINO

Here's my plan B!

Olivia will not see my face

So you will see her in my place!

Tell her how I love her mind.

And body, and face, and how she is kind.

I'm sure you know the things to say

To make Olivia fall my way.

Just flash your eyes and pucker your lips.

VIOLA

Thank you, sire, for the tips!

DUKE ORSINO

I'll leave you now with Cupid's task.

VIOLA

My Lord, I'll do whatever you ask!

[DUKE ORSINO exits.]

[Aside] As an honourable girl, I'll do it, see!

But I wish that he was wooing me!

SCENE V.

Olivia's house

[Enter MARIA and Clown]

MARIA
Oh Fool, you're back. Where did you go?
Olivia will have you hung, you know!

CLOWN
Where I went it doesn't matter.
I'll calm her down with my clever patter.

MARIA
If you're so smart, then why a fool?

Clown
I didn't get good marks at school.
A man must do what he knows best.
I'm smart enough to joke and jest!

MARIA
When Olivia comes, your head she'll smack!

Clown
And here she is . . .!

[Enter OLIVIA with MALVOLIO]

. . . your fool is back!

OLIVIA
Remove the fool who's acting shady.

Clown
[To MALVOLIO] Did you not hear? Take away the Lady.

OLIVIA
Why am I the fool? Do tell!

Clown
Your brother's soul does lie in hell!

OLIVIA
It lies in heaven I'll have you know!

Clown
Then why are you still mourning so?

OLIVIA
[A modest smile] Not bad. Malvolio, what do you say?
Shall we let the rascal stay?

MALVOLIO
A fool, at least, should make me smile.
This one has no wit or style.
I saw him lose a bout of wits
To no more than a group of twits.

OLIVIA
If to fools you are unkind
Then you've really lost your mind.

The feeblest mind has not the jester
But the man in which his jibes do fester!

CLOWN
Your comments, ma'am, do warm my heart.

OLIVIA
Don't overplay your little part!

[Re-enter MARIA]

MARIA
A young man waits to speak to you.

OLIVIA
Duke Orsino?

MARIA
    I know not who.
He's fair of face and fine in robe,
And speaking with your Uncle Tobe.

OLIVIA
Go spare him what my uncle thinks.
No doubt he's had a couple of drinks!

[Exit MARIA]

Malvolio, do now all you can
To get the lowdown on that man.
If he comes from Orsino,
Tell him that he's got to go!

[Exit MALVOLIO]

[Enter SIR TOBY BELCH]

OLIVIA
Uncle Toby, what a surprise!
You were late to bed?

SIR TOBY BELCH
    But early to rise!

OLIVIA
Are you drunk, Sir Toby?

SIR TOBY BELCH
    What a suggestion!
[Belches] It's just a little indigestion

CLOWN
Good Sir Toby! Why are you here?
[Pause] The man outside . . .?

SIR TOBY BELCH
[Pause] I've no idea!
Must be a little memory lapse!

OLIVIA
Take him, Fool, for one of his naps.

[Exit Clown and SIR TOBY BELCH]

[Re-enter MALVOLIO]

MALVOLIO
The boy is from Lord Orsino.

I told him that he had to go.
I said that you were feeling peaky.
He said I lied!

OLIVIA
> That's very cheeky!

MALVOLIO
He's ill of manner but not uncouth.

OLIVIA
And how old is he, this roguish youth?

MALVOLIO
Not yet a man, but not a boy
With silver tongue and strangely coy;

OLIVIA
Very well, I am keen to see
This messenger.

[Exit MALVOLIO]

[Calling] Come here, Marie.

[Re-enter MARIA]

OLIVIA
Put a veil upon my eyes
To give my person some disguise.

[Enter VIOLA]

VIOLA
Please show me where's Olivia?

OLIVIA
[Veiled] I am standing in for her.

VIOLA
Please show me her, I do beseech
It took me hours to learn my speech!

OLIVIA
Tell me from where did you arise?

VIOLA
I'm not allowed to improvise.
I have my lines. Now, where is she?

OLIVIA
Oh very well, the lady's me.

VIOLA
My master will be very happy!

OLIVIA
Just start your speech and make it snappy!

VIOLA
Just one more thing . . . a little space?

[To MARIA who moves away]

MARIE
I'll just be over here, your Grace.

OLIVIA
From where come the words of the speech you will start?

VIOLA
From me to you . . . via Orsino's heart.
I'm told to say them to your face.
Could you lift the veil, your Grace?

OLIVIA
You know it's me, no need to hide

[Unveiling]

You like the look of what's inside?

VIOLA
Well that, my dear, was worth the wait.
Your beauty explains Orsino's fate.
He sighs, he moans, he must be seen.

OLIVIA
He's nothing but a drama queen!
He knew my answer long ago.

VIOLA
Your cruel words will hurt him so.
If I got such a cruel reply,
I'd lie awake each night and cry.
I'd pitch a tent outside your gate
And evermore I'd sit and wait
For you to leave your icy heart.
All other plans I'd tear apart!

OLIVIA
You'd do all that?

VIOLA
   I have no doubt!

OLIVIA
Just take this money and get out!

VIOLA
I did not come here for a fee.
I could not buy such cruelty
That you do show my suffering Duke!

OLIVIA
That's a pretty strong rebuke.
Now strongly tell him, we are done!

VIOLA
I will, my Lady, but it won't be fun!

[Exit VIOLA]

OLIVIA
His master I will see no more.
But that young man I do adore.

[Removing a ring from her finger].

Malvolio, my stoic aide.

[Re-enter MALVOLIO]

Do a favour for this maid.
That boy he dropped this ring, you see?

[Gives the ring to MALVOLIO]

So track him down and say from me
To come tomorrow with his views
On how his master took my news.
And don't be angry, just be calm!

MALVOLIO
Forever at your service, Ma'am!

[Exit MALVOLIO]

Act II

The seacoast

[Enter ANTONIO and SEBASTIAN]

ANTONIO
My handsome sir, you cannot stay?

SEBASTIAN
Antonio, I must away.
The three months we've had have been quite jolly
But now I'm filled with melancholy.
If I do not leave right now from here,
Your love for me will disappear!

ANTONIO
Then leave me with some exposition
Before you start your lonely mission!

SEBASTIAN
The man you pulled out from the sea
Was Sebastian . . . that's me,
A nobleman from Messaline.
Until recently a twin I'd been.

But the storm that hit us out at sea
Took my sister Viola from me.

ANTONIO
A tragic tale of derring-do!
Tell me, your sister she looked like you?

SEBASTIAN
Identical we are.

ANTONIO
    You were!

SEBASTIAN
But she, of course, was prettier.

ANTONIO
My poor sweet boy, don't go alone.
Let me be your chaperone.

SEBASTIAN
To survive alone I at least should try.
This has to be our last goodbye.
I leave for Count Orsino's court,
To hide my pain with royal sport.
[Exit]

ANTONIO
I'd follow you if I could dare.
But once I got in trouble there.
It's dangerous now for me to follow,
But if I don't, I'll die of sorrow.

[Exit]

 SCENE II.

A street

[Enter VIOLA, MALVOLIO following]

MALVOLIO
Were you just with Olivia?

VIOLA
Why worry 'bout such trivia?

MALVOLIO
You left a ring, she gives it back

> *[Offers the ring]*

Your visit, I must say, was slack.
Such a cheap and tacky move.
Duke Orsino she will never approve.
She says that you can't come again
Unless to report your master's pain.

VIOLA
I had no ring on me, I swear.

MALVOLIO
Oh come, young man, you left it there.
She's returning it, just to be kind.

I'll leave it here. it's quite a find!

[Exit]

VIOLA
I left no ring: what does this mean?
I think on me she must be keen!
I knew this was a good disguise
But now I think it not so wise.
Cos she loves me, and I love him,
And he loves her; it all looks grim!
I'd like to get back in a dress!
But only time can solve this mess.

[Exit]

SCENE III.

Olivia's house

[Enter SIR TOBY BELCH and SIR ANDREW]

SIR TOBY BELCH
Come in, Sir Andrew, it's rude to wait.

SIR ANDREW
I was worried I was a little late.

SIR TOBY BELCH
Nonsense, sir. Midnight has passed.
Now everything's early.

SIR ANDREW
    And long may it last!

[Enter Clown]

Clown
May I join the early birds?

SIR TOBY BELCH
Put some music to your words!
Here is sixpence . . .

Clown

You're buying a song?

Sixpence worth of music. This won't take long!

SIR TOBY BELCH

Let's sing and do the roaming dance.

We'll wake up all from here to France.

SIR ANDREW

I'll sing like a dog.

Clown

I'll bark like a hound.

SIR TOBY BELCH

And I'll howl like a wolf to bring all the girls 'round. *[He howls drunkenly]*

Clown

[Singing to the tune of 'The Wild Rover']

Oh come pretty girlies and give us a kiss.

Don't think of the future, the future's amiss.

We don't want a missus, we just want some fun!

And we'll all be hungover when the kissing is done.

And it's oh nay never

When the kissing is done,

Don't think of the future, the future is dumb!

[Enter MARIA]

MARIA

What the hell is this noise?

SIR TOBY BELCH
> I told you my song
> Would bring in the ladies.

SIR ANDREW
> My friend, you weren't wrong!

MARIA
> The lady she did hear you shout,
> And if you do it again, she'll kick you all out!

SIR TOBY BELCH
> She won't do that; We're kith and kin!

MARIA
> Look out, Malvolio's coming in.

SIR ANDREW
> His sense of humour's been mislaid.

SIR TOBY BELCH
> That pompous poop we'll serenade.

[Enter MALVOLIO]

MALVOLIO
> Olivia was woken by a terrible din.
> Her house you've turned into an inn.
> You've all forgotten your whereabouts
> And behave like a bunch of drunken louts.
> Where's your wit? Your charm? Your grace?
> You've lost it all!

SIR TOBY BELCH
> Oh shut your face!

MALVOLIO
The drink has gotten the better of you.

SIR TOBY BELCH
It would do you good to have a few.

Clown
It would loosen you up; you're stiff as a brick.

SIR ANDREW
And he acts all posh, but really he's thick!

MALVOLIO
The pot does call the kettle black!
I speak for the lady, so have no doubt . . .

SIR TOBY BELCH
That's my niece you're talking about!

MALVOLIO
. . . When I say her patience is wearing thin

MARIA
For our love of her, we will lower our din!

SIR TOBY BELCH
Malvolio, you pompous git;
You're big of head, and short of wit.
You think you are so virtuous
That you can lord it over us?

Clown
As soon as you've gone, we will party again!

SIR TOBY BELCH
So run along and rub your chain!
Maria! Open a bottle of wine!

MALVOLIO
If you want to, that's just fine!
But just a little trivia,
I'm reporting to Olivia.
She does not appreciate this kind of thing,
And I will tell her everything!

[Exit]

SIR TOBY BELCH
Oh go, wiggle your ears!

SIR ANDREW
He's pretentious and dim.
I'd love to make a fool of him!

MARIA
Boys! Be patient and not uncouth.
Our lady is nervous since meeting some youth.
It's made her tense, and Malvolio too,
He's easy pickings for you know who!

SIR TOBY BELCH
So what is he like?

MARIA

A puritan.

SIR ANDREW

I'll beat him for that.

SIR TOBY BELCH

You can't!

SIR ANDREW

I can!

MARIA

But he's really not that good or pure.
He's just puffed up and insecure,
A flatterer and social snob
And he's only got a servant's job!
He thinks he's better than the rest of us
And that the lady thinks he is worth a fuss.
With all these flaws I know that we
Can bring him down a peg . . . or three!

SIR TOBY BELCH

So what's the plan?

SIR ANDREW

What's on your mind?

MARIA

I'll write love letters for him to find!
They'll describe the colour of his beard,
His legs, his face, but they won't seem weird.
Cos I'll write them in my lady's hand.

He will completely misunderstand!

SIR TOBY BELCH
Excellent! A clever ruse.

SIR ANDREW
That's the plan that we should choose!

SIR TOBY BELCH
His pride will spill right over his brim!
He'll think my niece's in love with him.

MARIA
And we will go and lie in wait
To watch him find the note.

SIR ANDREW
    That's great!

SIR TOBY BELCH
It's a cunning plan with a touch of class
That will have our man look like an arse!

MARIA
Now as for tonight, it's time for bed
To dream of the fun we have ahead.

[Exit]

SIR TOBY BELCH
Can you lend me more money?

SIR ANDREW

    I'll send for some more,

But if I don't wed Olivia, I'll be bankrupt for sure.

SIR TOBY BELCH

Don't you worry about that, my friend.

You'll win her over in the end.

SIR ANDREW

If I do, I'll die rich and merry.

SIR TOBY BELCH

Now it's too late for bed. Let's open the sherry!

[Exeunt]

SCENE IV.

Duke Orsino's palace

[Enter DUKE ORSINO, VIOLA and CURIO]

DUKE ORSINO
Give me some music. That song from last night
It helped distract me from my plight.

[CURIO plays]

[To VIOLA] When you fall in love; as you just might,
Unable to sleep, no appetite,
Thinking of your lover's face,
Just generally feeling, all over the place.
You'll feel like me. No one's immune.
What do you think of this little tune?

VIOLA
It makes me feel what a lover might feel.

DUKE ORSINO
And tell me, lad, have you felt that for real?

VIOLA
Just a little.

DUKE ORSINO
Describe her my page.

VIOLA
A little like you.

DUKE ORSINO
And what was her age?

VIOLA
Not much, like yours!

DUKE ORSINO
Yes, choose someone younger,
Someone with a bit of hunger
And energy to adapt to you.
I think that's key.

VIOLA
I think so too!
Someone who's surely in their prime.

DUKE ORSINO
Oh how I wish for a simpler time
When women were women . . .

VIOLA
And men were men?

[Enter Clown, hungover]

Oh here's that little clown again.

Clown

[Singing to the tune of 'The Wild Rover']

I feel myself dying, so gather round
And put my old body deep down in the ground.
Prepare me a shroud and a branch from the tree.
That beautiful girl she has gone and killed me.
And its no nay never, no nay never no more.
I've been killed by her beauty
You can all be sure!

DUKE ORSINO
[Giving the Clown a coin] A strange choice of music,
    neither happy nor long.

Clown
[Opening his hand to see the coin] Sixpence again! Did I do
    something wrong?
Maybe next time a ditty more jolly?

DUKE ORSINO
I take pleasure from your melancholy.
Now leave us here.

[Exit]

    Cesario!
To Olivia again you'll go!

The song from the Clown has made me brave.
So speak again for me, young knave!
Tell her that I know she is rich,
But I'd love her still if she hadn't a stitch.

VIOLA
But what if she just can't love you?

DUKE ORSINO
I can't believe that could be true!
My love is mighty like the sea.
It'll swallow her up, believe you me!
A female love is weaker than ours.
It can be bought with chocolates and flowers.

VIOLA
I may just beg to differ there.
My father's daughter, very fair,
She loved a man (and this may sound silly)
As I may love you . . . if I were a filly!

DUKE ORSINO
What happened to her?

VIOLA
     Her love was so strong
But unrequited. She didn't last long

[Awkward pause]

Shall I go to the lady?

DUKE ORSINO
     Yes, take her this jewel.

[Gives VIOLA a jewel]

Say I'm not going anywhere, I'm a lovesick young fool!

[Exeunt]

CENE V.

Olivia's garden

[Enter SIR TOBY BELCH, SIR ANDREW, and FABIAN]

SIR TOBY BELCH
Young Fabian? Servant?

FABIAN
I beg your pardon?

SIR TOBY BELCH
How lucky for you that you're here in the garden.

FABIAN
What's happening, Sir Toby? Is there a show?

SIR ANDREW
We're taking down Malvolio!

FABIAN
He always calls my fun a sin.

SIR TOBY BELCH
Well stick around, the joke's on him.

SIR ANDREW
And here she is, the mastermind!

[Enter MARIA]

MARIA
Behind this tree, if you'd be so kind.
Malvolio is on his way.
He's been practicing his manners all day.
Now not a peep, you all must hide.
I'll lay these letters in his stride.

[MARIA places the letters and exits]

SIR TOBY BELCH
This will be such an easy job.

FABIAN
He's such a daft pretentious snob.

SIR ANDREW
His manners are both trite and fickle,
Here comes the old trout, let's give him a tickle.

[Enter MALVOLIO, speaking to himself]

MALVOLIO
Maria did state on Olivia's behalf
That I am her favourite member of staff.
It's really no surprise that she
Is really rather taken with me!

SIR ANDREW
Deluded fool.

SIR TOBY BELCH
His mind is slack.

FABIAN
And such an egomaniac.

SIR ANDREW
I'll beat the rogue!

SIR TOBY BELCH
Sir Andrew, no!

MALVOLIO
They'll call me Count Malvolio!
I won't be the first to marry my way
From a servant to royalty, that I dare say.

FABIAN
Look how he dreams.

SIR ANDREW
Such pretentious a tone.
For a man so skilled at living alone!

MALVOLIO
And after three months married, I'll be the state's head,
Surrounded with servants, Olivia in bed . . .

SIR TOBY BELCH
Fire and brimstone!

FABIAN
Calm thee, man!

MALVOLIO
Handing out judgments as only I can ...
I'll call Uncle Toby.

SIR TOBY BELCH
 Oh will he? We'll see!

MALVOLIO
I'll act all aloof as he courtesies to me.

SIR TOBY BELCH
I'll kill the old goat for this story he's spun.

FABIAN
Just let him continue and don't spoil the fun.

MALVOLIO
I'll offer my ring which he will then kiss.

SIR TOBY BELCH
I'll punch him in the chops!

MALVOLIO
 Like this,
'Sir Toby', I'll say, with my newfound prestige,
'You must give up your drinking, I do you besiege!'

SIR TOBY BELCH
I'll give up my temper.

MALVOLIO
 'You're a waster, you see
And you drink with a moron.'

SIR ANDREW
He's talking about me!

MALVOLIO
'The fool that is Sir Aguecheek'.

SIR ANDREW
I knew he was!

SIR TOBY BELCH
[To SIR ANDREW] Your mind is weak!

MALVOLIO
What's this I see? A mysterious letter?

[Taking up the letter]

FABIAN
This just keeps getting better and better.

SIR TOBY BELCH
For the love of God, let him read it aloud.

MALVOLIO
It's my lady's handwriting!

SIR TOBY BELCH
Already he's proud

MALVOLIO
[Reads the envelope] 'To my unknown beloved, with all my heart'.
It's sealed with her ring; it's a very good start.
I'll open it. I cannot wait.

FABIAN
The fish is hooked.

SIR ANDREW
    He took the bait!

MALVOLIO

[Reads]

'I love a man, but no one must know'.
Well, that could be Malvolio!
'I may command who I adore
But silence does my poor heart gore
Without a knife, in a bloodless fashion
M.O.A.I. commands my passion'.

FABIAN
It's an awful tease and he should know it.

SIR TOBY BELCH
Maria is an excellent poet.

MALVOLIO
The Lady adores to whom she writes.
Well, clearly, I'm within her sights.
For years I've been right by her side
Will I take her for my bride?
Does she foresee a great romance?

SIR TOBY BELCH
I think I'm going to pee my pants!

MALVOLIO
And what about this final bit
M.O.A.I.?

SIR ANDREW
    We'll judge his wit

MALVOLIO
Well M could be Malvolio,
And the end of my name could be the O.
But the A remains a mystery
With an 'I' at the back . . .

SIR TOBY BELCH
    Of your head, you could see,
That you are being played, my friend.

MALVOLIO
There is some more writing, this isn't the end . . .

[Reads]

'If this letter is in your hands,
Follow carefully its commands.
By birth, I am a bit of a toff[1]
But don't let that fact put you off.
Some are born great, some greatness achieve
And greatness for others they simply receive.
The high life awaits you. Make changes, it's urgent:
Argue with relatives and be rude to a servant!
Talk about politics, think outside the box,

---

1   Derogatory British idiom for a rich or noble person

Show me you love me, wear yellow socks.

I hate to ask and I'll never beg

But wear crisscrossing laces that go right up your leg.

A new life awaits you, most grand and not crappy.

Yours sincerely, my love, signed The Fortunate Unhappy!'

What could be clearer? It's easy to see,

I'm as light as a feather. The lady loves me.

I recall she liked my yellow tights.

I'll wear them now for days and nights!

I'll baffle Sir Toby and ditch my old chums

And embrace the fate that this way comes.

From today, I'll be cultured in manners and dress,

The ying to her yang . . . *[Looking at the letter]* Oh, here's PS

[Reading] 'To let me know that you've deciphered this
    letter,

Walk around with a smile, or a grin, even better.

I'll know this is true and I am not simply dreaming

Whenever you're near me, your face it is beaming!'.

I can't believe it. My dream has come true!

Whatever the woman wants, I'll do.

[Exit]

FABIAN
I would not have missed this for a million quid.[2]

SIR TOBY BELCH
I'll marry Maria for what she just did.

---

2   British term for silver pounds.

SIR ANDREW
What a gem, what a legend!

FABIAN
> What a wonderful hoax!

> *[Re-enter MARIA]*

SIR TOBY BELCH
And here is the queen of the practical jokes!
Your letter it worked!

MARIA
> I am ever so glad!

SIR ANDREW
When he finds out the truth, he'll go stark-raving mad!

MARIA
You think that that's funny? You wait for a while
Till he wears yellow stockings and a big stupid smile.
My mistress hates yellow and continues to mourn.
With his socks and his grinning, she will pour on him
> scorn.
So stick with me to see her attack.

SIR TOBY BELCH
We'd follow you to hell and back.

> *[Exeunt]*

Act III

 SCENE I.

Olivia's garden

[Enter VIOLA and Clown with a tabour]

VIOLA
Good day, young sir, you live by your drum?

Clown
I live by the church.

VIOLA
    You are a churchman?

Clown
No, the church is literally next to my place.

VIOLA
Your playing with words brings a smile to my face!

Clown
I never mean to cause offense,
But the one thing I share with the church is . . . a fence.

VIOLA
I'm admiring of your grammatical tricks,
But when playing with words their meaning you mix.

Clown
That's my job.

VIOLA
You're a Jester! Olivia's jolly?

Clown
Until she is married, she's got no time for folly.
Occasionally I'm there when I follow my nose.

VIOLA
Didn't I see you once at Count Orsino's?

Clown
Foolery, sir, has an unquenchable thirst.

VIOLA
I did see you there.

Clown
But I saw you there first!

VIOLA
Here's a coin for your humour.

Clown

God send thee a beard!

To be bare-faced at your age is verging on weird.

VIOLA

Oh I'm dying for one *[Aside]* But not of my own!

Now tell me, young jester, is Olivia home?

Clown

[Looking at the coin] I would go in and check if my coin had
a mate.

VIOLA

[Giving him another coin]

You cheeky young beggar, now go in! I'll wait!

[Clown exits]

VIOLA

He's wise enough to play a fool.

They sure don't teach you that at school.

The more foolish he is, the wiser he seems.

But a wise man can come apart at the seams!

[Enter SIR TOBY BELCH and SIR ANDREW]

SIR TOBY BELCH

Good day, good sir.

VIOLA

And you.

SIR ANDREW
Bonjour!

VIOLA
Et vous aussi.[3]

SIR ANDREW
About twenty past four!
What are you doing? Do you wait for a bus?

SIR TOBY BELCH
If you're here for my niece, you may enter with us.

VIOLA
I am here for her, sir.

SIR TOBY BELCH
Then your legs you must taste.

VIOLA
[Confused] Do you mean by that, I should enter with
haste?

SIR TOBY BELCH
You should enter with us.

VIOLA
But the gate it is closed.

[Enter OLIVIA and MARIA]

Oh beautiful lady, how well you're disposed!

---

3   "And you as well" in French.

SIR ANDREW
'How well you're disposed!' He's a silver tongue!

VIOLA
For your delicate ear should my message be sung.

OLIVIA
Take my hand; we will enter. You others stay here.

SIR TOBY BELCH
I think she is smitten.

SIR ANDREW
    You're right there, I fear.

[Exeunt SIR TOBY BELCH, SIR ANDREW, and MARIA]

OLIVIA
Now tell me your name. I really must know.

VIOLA
Your servant's name's . . . Cesario.

OLIVIA
Oh don't talk nonsense. You're Orsino's *man.*

VIOLA
But his servant's servant is your servant, ma'am.
And he worships you.

OLIVIA
    I couldn't care less.
Let's talk about us.

VIOLA About what?

OLIVIA
Can't you guess?
The last time we parted, you left with my heart.
So I sent you my servant with a ring to impart.
I lied, I was desperate, and I wanted you back.
I'd closed up my heart, but you fell through a crack.
Now what do you think? Would you say I am pretty?
Could there be love? Maybe more?

VIOLA
I feel pity!

OLIVIA
Pity is love's nursery!

VIOLA
I pity my adversary!

OLIVIA
Then it's time to let you go.
A foolish heart I did you show.
No such right I had to love.
At least you're gentle, like a dove.

[Clock strikes]

You may be a corker,
But I won't be your stalker.
And when you get to marry, she
Will be so lucky, unlike me.
And now you must go westward-ho.

VIOLA
With nothing for poor Duke Orsino?

OLIVIA
Give me your opinion before you go far.

VIOLA
I think that you think you are not what you are.

OLIVIA
If that's true you're the same; I think you're a sham.

VIOLA
And you're right to think that: I am not what I am.

OLIVIA
I wish you were what I thought you were.

VIOLA
I'm starting to think with your view I concur,
Cos right now I am feeling a bit of a twit.

OLIVIA
[Aside] He's even attractive when he's being a git.
[With passion] My guilty love I cannot hide.
Cesario, let me be your bride!
You've stolen from me my grace and poise.
And I don't say that to all the boys!
Your longing for me would be such a treat.
And I'm not averse to kissing your feet!

VIOLA
It doesn't matter what you say.

I'll never see you in that way.
I have one heart, one bosom, and one head,
And a woman will never share my bed.
If that means I will always be single,
So be it, dear, I'm off to mingle.
Goodbye, good lady, and never more
Will I come for my master to darken your door.

OLIVIA
Please return; you never know.
She who he loves in your heart may grow!

[Exeunt]

$\mathcal{S}$CENE II

Olivia's house

[Enter SIR TOBY BELCH, SIR ANDREW, and FABIAN]

SIR ANDREW
That's it! I'm off! I'm out of here.

SIR TOBY BELCH
But what's your reason?

FABIAN
    Come, say it clear!

SIR ANDREW
I was watching your niece in the garden just now.
She was flirting with some youth, and how!

SIR TOBY BELCH
Did she see you?

SIR ANDREW
    Don't know! I was near the big tree.

FABIAN
Well, that was your opportunity!

SIR TOBY BELCH
She was clearly trying to make you feel jealous!

FABIAN
You should have jumped out all fiery and zealous,
Beat up the kid then shown her your dance,
Told a few jokes! That was your big chance!
You looked a gift horse in the mouth.
Now your chances with her could have all gone south!

SIR TOBY BELCH
Unless! [Pause] You challenge the youth to a fight!
When you beat up that squirt, she will see your true
    might.

FABIAN
She'll be like putty in your hands.

SIR TOBY BELCH
And very receptive to all your demands!

SIR ANDREW
I hope you are not just toying with me!

FABIAN
We are both on your side.

SIR TOBY BELCH
    Obviously!

SIR ANDREW
Will one of you go and challenge him then?

SIR TOBY BELCH
No, no, Sir Andrew, it should come from your pen.
Make it brief but elaborate, concise but with pith.
Leave him in no doubt who he's dealing with.
Give the impression you are harsh and unpleasant.

SIR ANDREW
I'll go make a start.

SIR TOBY BELCH
No time like the present.

[Exit SIR ANDREW]

FABIAN
To you, he is a mannequin.

SIR TOBY BELCH
It's far too easy; it's really a sin!

FABIAN
A sin it's as maybe, but it's still very funny.

SIR TOBY BELCH
I need him around to drink all his money!

FABIAN
But you won't deliver his letter, of course.

SIR TOBY BELCH
I will not be stopped by the wildest horse!
But even if we get a reply,
They'll never stand there eye to eye.

I know for a fact that Sir Andrew is yellow.

FABIAN
And the other guy looks like no fighting fellow!

[Enter MARIA]

SIR TOBY BELCH
And here she is, the queen of the japes!

MARIA
Close the windows, pull the drapes,
Drop everything, and follow me,
The funniest thing you'll ever see.
Malvolio, he looks absurd.
He's done the lot.

SIR TOBY BELCH
     What? Every word?

MARIA
His yellow socks come up to his knee.
He looks like a big bumblebee.
With flaxen garters done up in a plait.
He's grinning like a Cheshire cat!
She'll strike him down, and he'll just smirk.
He looks like a demented jerk!
It's the funniest thing in the world, for sure!

SIR TOBY BELCH
Well come on, what are we waiting for?

[Exeunt]

SCENE III.

A street

[Enter SEBASTIAN and ANTONIO]

SEBASTIAN
I thought we said you'd stay on the beach.

ANTONIO
Don't punish me, I do beseech!
I was worried to death the moment you'd gone
To think that something in town could go wrong.
It's not the most hospitable place
For a polite young man with such a nice face.

SEBASTIAN
Alone I didn't want to go.
You're very sweet, Antonio.

ANTONIA
You know I'm very fond of you?

SEBASTIAN
I'm not surprised. I think I knew.
I'd give you a treat for coming with me,
If I hadn't lost all my possessions at sea.
But let not that fact get us down.

Let's go and have a look around.

You know the place, what's worth a look?

ANTONIO
I think we first a room should book.

SEBASTIAN
It's hours before the sun goes down.
Let's first just have a look around.

ANTONIO
I'll have to decline your offer, dear.
I've got a bit of history here.
Our cities had a bit of a fight.

SEBASTIAN
If your crimes were of war, then you'd better take flight!

ANTONIO
It was nothing so bad. I just owe them some loot.
But if they see me around, they will give me a boot.
I'll get us a room at the Elephant Pub.
It'll be safer up there and I'll order some grub.
Take your time and my money; buy something you'll
    treasure.

[Gives Sebastian money]

SEBASTIAN
Well, I don't need all that.

ANTONIO
    Yes you do. It's my pleasure.

It's something I want to do for you.

SEBASTIAN
You're too kind.

ANTONIO
   I insist.

SEBASTIAN
   Then what can I do?
You really are benevolent!

ANTONIO
I'll see you at The Elephant!

[Exeunt]

SCENE IV.

Olivia's garden

[Enter OLIVIA and MARIA]

OLIVIA
Cesario's agreed again to meet.
But what gifts shall I give? And what will he eat?
Where is Malvolio? He is sad and he's serious.
He always helps me from being delirious!

MARIA
He's coming but he's looking possessed.

OLIVIA
That's the last thing I need. I already feel stressed.
Is he fevered?

MARIA
　　No. ma'am, he does nothing but grin!

OLIVIA
We'll cure him of that, just go show him in.

[Exit MARIA]

If he's going crazy, I know how he feels.
I'm mourning my brother, yet I'm head over heels!

[Re-enter MARIA with a grinning yellow MALVOLIO]

How are you, dear Malvolio?

MALVOLIO
Never better, ho, ho, ho, ho!

OLIVIA
You're laughing? Please act soberly!

MALVOLIO
I should; these socks are killing me.
These laces hurt, they really do!
But it's worth it if they're pleasing you.
My mind is well and my legs are yellow.

OLIVIA
You're appearing like a crazy fellow.
Perhaps you need to go to bed?

MALVOLIO
I think *we* do!

OLIVIA
He's wrong in the head!

MARIA
[To MALVOLIO] Are you alright? You're strange
somehow.

MALVOLIO
I do not talk to servants now.

MARIA
You are so bold.

MALVOLIO
    I am so great!
Isn't that what you wrote? I'm fulfilling my fate!

OLIVIA
I'm missing something. *[Turning to MARIA]* Explain this
    please!

MALVOLIO
You want to stare at my bees-knees?
Well, go ahead, my dear. Feel free!

[Enter Servant]

SERVANT
Cesario's here, begrudgingly!
Shall I show him inside?

OLIVIA
    No, I'll come out of fear.

[Exit Servant]

Get my uncle to see banana-legs here.
And tell him to care for this strange fellow's health.
If he does, I'll share with him some of my wealth!

[Exeunt OLIVIA and MARIA]

MALVOLIO
With a stubborn grin and socks of yellow,

You heard her say I was her fellow.
And now she sends Sir Toby here.
A flea I'll put into his ear!
Just like the words she wrote in her letter.
From this point on, our lives only get better!
Our love is like a work of art.
Nothing now can keep us apart.

[Re-enter MARIA, with SIR TOBY BELCH and FABIAN]

SIR TOBY BELCH
I don't care if he's lost the plot.
I want to see now what is what.

FABIAN
Here he is, old smiley face!

MALVOLIO
Move away from my personal space.

MARIA
He looks like he has been possessed.

SIR TOBY BELCH
We must treat him with due gentleness.

[Performing a mock exorcism]

Just say no to bad Old Nick!⁴

---

4   A nickname for the Devil

MALVOLIO
Don't talk such rot!

MARIA
    He's very quick
To defend the devil over you!

FABIAN
I think I know what we should do.
We need to bring a doctor in!

MARIA
You've upset him with your talk of sin!

MALVOLIO
You speak, Maria?

MARIA
    Oh let me be!

SIR TOBY BELCH
Stand back and leave the man to me!

FABIAN
If you are kind, he won't resist.

SIR TOBY BELCH
I will be his exorcist!

    [Speaking to the devil inside MALVOLIO]

Come on out, you evil sprite!

MALVOLIO
Away from me!

SIR TOBY BELCH
    Come see the light!
Leave this man! Come seize the day!

MARIA
Good Sir Toby, get him to pray!

MALVOLIO
To pray? What for?

MARIA
    He shuns the Lord!

FABIAN
Shall we try the waterboard?

MALVOLIO
Go hang yourselves! You toy with me!
In time I'll teach you dignity.
[Exit]

SIR TOBY BELCH
He has indeed a weird affliction.

FABIAN
Sometimes the truth is stranger than fiction.

MARIA
He definitely thinks the letter was real
And he's playing his part with extraordinary zeal!

SIR TOBY BELCH
He should see through this joke with ease.

FABIAN
But there's plenty of sport left in this wheeze!

SIR TOBY BELCH
Let's lock him in a darkened den.

MARIA
The house will be much quieter then!

SIR TOBY BELCH
Maybe then he'll learn his lesson.
Then we will offer our confession.
Olivia already thinks he's mad.
We'll keep him there 'till our fun we've had.

[Enter SIR ANDREW]

FABIAN
Talking of which . . .

SIR ANDREW
        I've written the letter!
It's sharp and it's salty.

FABIAN
This day just gets better!
So it's saucy?

SIR ANDREW
        It is. Just read it and see.

SIR TOBY BELCH
I have no doubt. Now give it to me.
[Reads] 'You're nothing but a scurvy knave.
I don't like you'.

FABIAN
That's very brave.

SIR TOBY BELCH
[Reads] 'I won't say why'.

FABIAN
That's even braver.

SIR TOBY BELCH
[Reads] 'Olivia, you came to savour,
But you lied to her; she was honest and true.
But that's not why I am challenging you'.

FABIAN
Not to the point, but very brief!

SIR TOBY BELCH
[Reads] 'I will mug you like a common thief'.

FABIAN
That will shock him without fail.

SIR TOBY BELCH
[Reads] 'If you kill me first, you could go to jail'.

FABIAN
That's good, you will be blameless.

SIR TOBY BELCH

[Reads] 'May God not judge us shameless.

Look after yourself. Signed your friend, if you're nice.

Or if you are not, then your enemy-thrice'.

If this won't provoke him to fight you this week

Your name's not Sir Aguecheek!

I'll deliver it now with all good haste.

MARIA

The kid's with my lady, so no time to waste.

SIR TOBY BELCH

Go, Sir Andrew, and wait in the wood.

When he passes, you can scare him good!

Pull out your sword, then curse and swear.

And you may even avoid a fight right there!

Colourful language and a threatening pose

Can sometimes bring a feud to a close.

SIR ANDREW

I'm good at cursing as all of you know.

[Exit]

SIR TOBY BELCH

But no good with words, as this letter does show.

If I delivered this rag to the youth,

He would know that Sir Andrew's a fool and uncouth.

He wouldn't be scared, so it's better if I

Go and speak to the youth, man to man, eye to eye.

I will spin him some yarn before Andrew appears

So they'll only die of mutual fears.

[Re-enter OLIVIA with VIOLA]

FABIAN
Here he is now with the lady once more.

SIR TOBY BELCH
I will wait till she leaves, then I'll scare him for sure.

[Exeunt SIR TOBY BELCH, FABIAN, and MARIA]

OLIVIA
I know I've said too much to you.
You've a stony heart. I'm a fool, that's true.
But I'm full of passion.

VIOLA
　　My master's the same.

OLIVIA
I give you this locket to cover my shame.
Refuse it not; it cannot speak.
And come and see me again this week.
What could you ask that I could not deny?

VIOLA
Only love for my Master.

OLIVIA
　　Oh! Now I will cry!
I gave that to you.

VIOLA
　　And I give it you back.

OLIVIA
Return here tomorrow! Your soul, sir, is black!

[Exit]

[Re-enter SIR TOBY BELCH and FABIAN]

SIR TOBY BELCH
God save thee, sir!

VIOLA
    [Confused] And God save you!

SIR TOBY BELCH
You need his help more than I do!
A knight is hiding in the copse.
He waits for you to bust your chops!

VIOLA
Are you sure it's me he's looking for?

SIR TOBY BELCH
One hundred percent. I would, therefore,
Grab all the fighting tools you've got.

VIOLA
Who is this man?

SIR TOBY BELCH
    He's got the lot!
He is a knight with a fearsome blade
He's killed three men, so be afraid!
Bodies and souls he separates

And in the woods for you he waits!

VIOLA

I'm sure I have done nothing to provoke such a bout.

But you can't be too careful, there are some weirdos
about!

I'll pop back in if that's alright with you.

And ask for an escort home or two!

SIR TOBY BELCH

I assure you his complaint is just.

So fight you will and fight you must.

Or take off that sword and lose your honour!

VIOLA

Just do me one favour, in case I'm a goner.

His reason and his arms sound strong.

Go ask the knight what I did wrong!

SIR TOBY BELCH

I'll do that for you because it sounds fair.

[To FABIAN]

Do not let him go anywhere!

[Exit]

VIOLA

Is this knight as bad as he makes out?

FABIAN

Well, he's not much to look at but he's fierce in a bout!

The most bloodthirsty knight in Illyria.

We could beg if it'll make you feel cheerier.

Let's go find him together!

VIOLA

That would make me feel brighter.

As you can see, I'm more lover than fighter!

[Exeunt]

[Re-enter SIR TOBY BELCH with SIR ANDREW]

SIR TOBY BELCH

Bad news on the man that you've challenged to fight.

It's like fighting three men in the dark of the night.

We had a quick spar and I'm telling you, man!

They say that he fought for the Shah of Iran!

SIR ANDREW

Stuff it then, I'll cancel it.

SIR TOBY BELCH

The man is chomping at the bit!

Fabian can't hold him back.

SIR ANDREW

I thought he was an anorak5!

I wish I knew that he was tough.

I'll offer my horse.

---

5   An anorak is a kind of winter coat. It is also British slang for a nerd.

SIR TOBY BELCH

That may be enough

[Aside] You ride your nag as I ride you.

[Re-enter FABIAN and VIOLA, VIOLA and SIR ANDREW do not notice each other]

[To VIOLA] Cesario! Don't look so blue!

[To FABIAN about SIR ANDREW] I've given him a right good scare.

[To VIOLA] To call off the bout he does offer his mare!

FABIAN

[To SIR TOBY] And my man's got St. Vitus' Dance!

He may well need to change his pants!

SIR TOBY BELCH

[To SIR ANDREW] The bad news is he's set on this bout.

VIOLA

And the good news?

SIR TOBY BELCH

Is that he won't take you out.

He's realised you didn't mean any offense,

So there's no need to offer him any defence.

Just draw your sword to make it look right

And that will be the end of the fight!

VIOLA

[Aside] If this does not all go to plan

I'll have to tell them I'm not a man!

*[SIR TOBY and FABIAN encourage VIOLA and SIR
ANDREW towards each other]*

SIR TOBY BELCH
[To SIR ANDREW] Come, Sir Andrew, the man is
　　resolved.

A duel, not a horse, will get this solved.

But he has promised me as a gentleman.

He'll go easy on you; well as much as he can!

SIR ANDREW
I'll give it a go but I'm feeling ill!

VIOLA
I'm doing this against my will!

[They draw their swords and waft them around a bit]

[Enter ANTONIO]

ANTONIO
Leave him alone!

SIR TOBY BELCH
　　What's this about?

ANTONIO
For this boy's love, I'll take you out!

SIR TOBY BELCH
You claim to be an undertaker?

Come over here and meet your maker.

[SIR TOBY and ANTONIO draw their swords]

[Enter Officers]

FABIAN
Look out, Sir Toby, the police have arrived.

SIR TOBY BELCH
[To ANTONIO] I'll deal with you later.

VIOLA
   I think I've survived!

SIR ANDREW
And to celebrate, I'll give you my steed.

FIRST OFFICER
[Pointing to ANTONIO] Is this the man?

SECOND OFFICER
   It is indeed.
I arrest you now, Antonio
For stealing stuff from Orsino.

ANTONIO
Unhand me, sir, it's a disgrace!

FIRST OFFICER
Oh no it's not.

SECOND OFFICER
   We know your face!

ANTONIO
That was years ago! It won't happen again.

FIRST OFFICER
That's very true! You're off to the pen!

ANTONIO
[Surrendering] Alright, alright, whatever you say.
[To VIOLA] But just before they take me away,
In order for things not to get worse.
I'm sorry to ask, but please give me my purse.

SECOND OFFICER
Don't think of trying anything funny!

ANTONIO
[To VIOLA] I must entreat you for some of that money.

VIOLA
What money, sir?

ANTONIO
     You'll deny me now?
After all we've been through? I don't know how!

VIOLA
This whole thing just seems very strange.
I can offer you a little change.

ANTONIO
After all the generous things I have done?

VIOLA
I'm racking my brains to think of one.

ANTONIO
O heaven forbid!

SECOND OFFICER
 Just save your breath.

ANTONIO
I snatched him from the jaws of death.
I showed him love and rare devotion.

VIOLA
Wherever did you get that notion?

FIRST OFFICER
He obviously doesn't know you sir

ANTONIO
Sebastian, a man you were!
But your handsome looks do hide a soul
As cold as ice, as black as coal.
The cruellest sorts are those that hide
Below their beauty the devil inside!

VIOLA
You've got a vivid imagination.

FIRST OFFICER
Which we'll hear about back at the station!

ANTONIO
Happily, I'll go with you

[Exit with Officers]

VIOLA
[Aside] He seems to think his words are true.
He called me by my brother's name.
Could he be thinking I am the same?

SIR TOBY BELCH
[To SIR ANDREW and FABIAN] Come on boys, the party's
    done.
Let's go start another one!

VIOLA
[Aside] The way I'm dressed and use my wit,
I am indeed my brother's spit.
So unless that man was out of his head,
My brother Sebastian is no longer dead.

[Exit]

SIR TOBY BELCH
What a very dishonest and paltry kid
For dumping his friend the way that he did.

SIR ANDREW
Next time around, I will beat him plain.

SIR TOBY BELCH
Just never try using your weapon again!

FABIAN
Let's set up the next duel once we've had a breather.

SIR TOBY BELCH
And I bet on my life, that won't happen either.

[Exeunt]

Act IV

SCENE I.

Before Olivia's house.

[Enter SEBASTIAN and Clown]

Clown
I've got the wrong man?

SEBASTIAN
    That's what I just said!

Clown
I suppose then that Cesario's dead
And my lady doesn't ask for you?

SEBASTIAN
Please vent your folly somewhere new!

Clown
'Vent my folly!' You're a poet my friend!

Shall I 'vent' to my lady that you will attend?

SEBASTIAN
Here is a coin, and move on cos I'm bored
Or I'll 'vent' to you with the tip of my sword!

Clown

[Looking at the coin]

He may well be a gentleman.

[Enter SIR ANDREW, SIR TOBY BELCH, and FABIAN]

SIR ANDREW
Aha you rogue, we meet again?

[Striking SEBASTIAN]

I'll cure you of your cocky swagger.

SIR TOBY BELCH
Stop right there or you'll lose your dagger.

Clown
I'll go straight in and tell my miss.
They'll all be in big trouble for this.

[Exit]

SIR TOBY BELCH

[Grabbing SEBASTIAN]

Stop fighting, sir.

SEBASTIAN
No. Leave me be.

[Drawing his sword]

Come on big man and fight with me.

SIR TOBY BELCH
If I did that, I'd take from you
A pint of your blood . . . or even two!

[Enter OLIVIA]

OLIVIA
Uncle Toby!

SIR TOBY BELCH
Oh here we go!

OLIVIA
I'm sorry, dear Cesario.
All three of you get out of my sight.

[Exeunt SIR TOBY BELCH, SIR ANDREW, and FABIAN]

Now tell me, dear, are you alright?
Come with me now, back to my house,
I'll tell you stories of that louse.
And all the things he's failed to do,
They'll put you in a better hue.

SEBASTIAN
[Aside] What madness is this? It's not every day
That an offer from someone like this comes my way.

I may be mad or this may be a scheme:
Just don't wake me up if I'm having a dream!

OLIVIA
Will you come with me?

SEBASTIAN
    I'm in your hands.

OLIVIA
If only you were, I've got such big plans!

[Exeunt]

SCENE II.

Olivia's house

[Enter MARIA and Clown]

MARIA
Wear this gown and beard. And until this joke's ceased,
You'll pretend to be Sir Topas, a priest!

[Exit]

[Enter SIR TOBY BELCH]

SIR TOBY BELCH
[To Clown] Father Topas, God bless you!
I think you know what you have to do!
We've locked him in this darkened room

Clown

[Calling as a priest]

I come and bring peace to this tomb!

SIR TOBY BELCH
[Aside] The clown does well.

MALVOLIO
[Within] Who's there? What ho!

Clown
Sir Topas for Malvolio.

MALVOLIO
Sir Topas, Sir Topas, my lady, my lady!

Clown
He talks only of women; it's alarming.

SIR TOBY BELCH
      And shady!

MALVOLIO
Sir Topas, I am not unwell.
They've locked me in this darkened cell.

Clown
It doesn't look too dark to me.
It's the devil preventing you to see.

MALVOLIO
Tell me what's the difference?

Clown
Darkness is but ignorance!

MALVOLIO
This room's as dark as humanity
Please test me on my sanity!

Clown
What did Pythagoras say about fowl?

MALVOLIO
That grandmas' souls inside them prowl.

Clown
Do you agree?

MALVOLIO
    He was blind as a bat.
My grandma's soul is nobler than that.

Clown
The Greek was one of those clear-sighted chaps,
And until you agree, you'll stay under wraps.
Fare thee well, Malvolio!

MALVOLIO
Stay with me, Topas, please don't go!

SIR TOBY BELCH
Sir Topas is the priest of the dark.

Clown
I'm very good at this acting lark.

MARIA
You didn't need to wear the disguise.
Down there he cannot use his eyes!

SIR TOBY BELCH
Now chat with him without deceit.

We really should put an end to this feat.
I'm already in enough hot water
With Olivia, my brother's daughter.
If he's well enough, we'll set him free.
Report to my room presently!

[Exeunt SIR TOBY BELCH and MARIA]

Clown

[Singing to the tune of 'The Wild Rover',
interrupted by MALVOLIO]

'Oh tell me my brother of the golden rule.
Keep and eye on your woman.'

MALVOLIO
Is that you there, Fool?

Clown

[Singing]

'Your lady's cold-hearted, plays you for a . . .'

MALVOLIO
Clown!

Clown

[Singing]

'She's loving another while you're not around.
And it's no nay never . . .'

MALVOLIO
Get me out of this jail!

Clown

[Singing]

'She loves another, as a lover you fail!'

MALVOLIO
Good fool, I beg you, don't sing that again.
Just bring me a candle some paper and pen.

Clown
Malvolio? Have you gone mad?

MALVOLIO
By no means sir, I've just been had!
I swear I am as sane as you.

Clown
As sane as a fool? Well that won't do.

MALVOLIO
They keep me locked up, without any lights.
Only churchmen to speak to, I've lost all my rights!

Clown
Watch what you're saying. The minister's back!

[As Topas]

Malvolio you've had a nasty attack.

MALVOLIO
Sir Topas!

Clown
    [As Topas to Clown] Speak with him no more!
[As Clown to Topas] I will not, Father, you can be sure.
As Topas to Clown] God bless you and Uncle Tobe.
[As Clown to Topas] I like your dress!
[As Topas to Clown] It's called a robe!

MALVOLIO
Wait up fool, please give me a pen.

Clown
I was told we shouldn't talk again.

MALVOLIO
If I write to Olivia,
I'll hire you as deliverer.

Clown
Are you sure you're well?

MALVOLIO
    I'm as sane as thee.

Clown
You might be just pretending to be!

MALVOLIO
Believe me, I'm not, that's a Catch-22!

Clown

I'll go get a pen and bring it to you.

[Singing to the tune of 'The Wild Rover']

I am gone, I am leaving, but I will be back

To help get your body from out of the black.

As a willing accomplice the devil I'll aid.

I know he is desperate, so the job is well paid.

And it's oh nay never, I'll be back with a pen

These priests make good money, I might do this again.

[Exit]

SCENE III.

Olivia's garden

[Enter SEBASTIAN]

SEBASTIAN
[Aside] Well what a turn-up for the books.
If this is all as good as it looks,
Then I really am living my dreams
But can it be as good as it seems?
Antonio would offer some useful advice,
But he's left the hotel, and I went back there twice.
I hope he's not in any trouble.
I'll wait for him in this gorgeous bubble
Of opulence, and not to mention
That beautiful woman who demands my attention.

[Enter OLIVIA and Priest]

OLIVIA
I see that you finally like what you see.

SEBASTIAN
It didn't take long, believe you me!

OLIVIA
For the first time I notice your cute Adam's apple.

Will you leave me now with the priest to the chapel?

I'll join you there shortly; we'll exchange our vows

And the town we'll tell later. *[Pause]* Do you raise your
eyebrows?

SEBASTIAN

If I'm honest it's come as a bit of a shock,

But if heaven's door opens there's no need to knock!

OLIVIA

Then Holy Father, lead him away

I'll join you for our wedding day!

[Exeunt]

Act V

SCENE I.

Before Olivia's house.

[Enter Clown and FABIAN]

FABIAN
Tell me good fool, what he says in his letter.

Clown
I assure you that nothing would make you feel better
Than reading this note.

> *[He looks like he will read it and then changes his mind.]*
> *But alas and alack.*

FABIAN
That's like giving a dog and then wanting it back.

> *[Enter DUKE ORSINO, VIOLA, CURIO, and Lords]*

DUKE ORSINO
You serve Lady Olivia?

Clown
    All our love we give to her!

DUKE ORSINO
I know thee, Clown, how meet you your ends?

Clown
Better from my foes and worse for my friends.

DUKE ORSINO
Don't you mean the other way around?

Clown
My friends are all liars, my enemies sound.
They say I'm a fool and say it plain
My friends say I'm normal but they think I'm insane!
From my foes, I learn the honest truth.
From my friends, I learn they are simply uncouth.

DUKE ORSINO
That's very smart.

Clown
    Don't say that stuff.
You sound like a friend. I've got more than enough!

DUKE ORSINO
I shan't be your friend; there's a gold coin for you

[Gives Clown another coin]

Clown
You should try double-dealing, I'd be better with two.

DUKE ORSINO
You encourage deception?

Clown
    You won't get in trouble.

DUKE ORSINO
For this, my amusement, I will gladly pay double.

[Gives Clown another coin]

Clown
Now what about the best of three?
That would really work for me.

DUKE ORSINO
The rules of sense you start to flout,
But you'll get your third if your mistress comes out

Clown
Then keep that third coin warm for me.
My Mistress will be here presently.

[Exit]

VIOLA
There's the man, sir, that rescued me.

[Enter ANTONIO and Officers]

DUKE ORSINO
I remember that face from a battle at sea.
He was captain of a tiny craft
That fought against us fore and aft.
We admired him then for being so strong,
So what on earth is going on?

FIRST OFFICER
You remember well, Duke Orsino.
The man's name is Antonio.

SECOND OFFICER
A salty and disreputable sort.
We questioned him and here's our report:

FIRST OFFICER
He took our cargo from your boat in Crete,
With lots of stuff, it was some feat.
He was wondering around without a care.
To be honest, I don't know how he dare.

VIOLA
He did me a kindness and saved me a fight.
Then started to rant; he didn't sound right.

DUKE ORSINO
Notable pirate! Salt-water thief!
That you came to our shores, it beggars belief!

ANTONIO
I admit I was your enemy,
But I stuck to laws of chivalry!

I visit your Illyria
Because of some deliria.
That boy, whose life I saved at sea,
Put some magic spell on me.
I gave him everything I had:
My love, my life, both good and bad,
And all my money. But yesterday,
I asked for some back and he refused to pay.
I saved his life, then I was arrested.
He disowned me. My case is rested!

VIOLA
How can this be? None of its true?
I do not have any memory of you!

DUKE ORSINO

[To ANTONIO]

When did you arrive in town, I beseech?

ANTONIO
Today, my lord; we were stuck on the beach.
For three long months until yesterday,
And out of our sight, neither did stray

[Enter OLIVIA and Attendants]

DUKE ORSINO
Here comes the countess; our angel appears.
And as for you villain, you damage my ears.
Three months this youth has been in my employ,
But more of this later. Move away from the boy.

OLIVIA
Good evening, Duke! Quite a crowd I see.
Now what do you need? And don't say me!
Hold that thought! Cesario!
You are not at the church; why did you not go?

VIOLA
[Confused] I'm sorry?

DUKE ORSINO
     My Lady?

OLIVIA
         [To Viola] Say something!

DUKE ORSINO
            [To Viola] Yes, speak!

VIOLA
You both demand, but I'm turning my cheek.

OLIVIA
If you speak with the same old tone as before,
Then words from now on I will only abhor.

DUKE ORSINO
Still so cruel?

OLIVIA
     I'm not so bad.

DUKE ORSINO
I gave you everything I had.

What else can I do? What do you suggest?

OLIVIA
Whatever you like, be my guest!

DUKE ORSINO
I should kill you first, then suicide
For not agreeing to be my bride,
But now he's *[Points to VIOLA]* stolen your heart away.
Maybe I've another play?
Although this boy is very nice,
He will be my sacrifice.
To spite this woman.

VIOLA

[To ORSINO]

I cannot lie.
If it makes you feel better, I will willingly die.

[Moves towards ORSINO]

OLIVIA
Where do you go, Cesario?

VIOLA
I love this man more than you know.
More than my eyes, and more than my life,
And certainly more than any old wife.

OLIVIA
I am broken! I'm beaten! I stand here defeated!

VIOLA
Why say you that, my Lady? You haven't been cheated.

OLIVIA
Do you not have a memory?
Bring the priest out here to me.

DUKE ORSINO
[Aiming to leave] Come along!

OLIVIA
　　[To VIOLA] My husband, stay.

DUKE ORSINO
Her husband!

OLIVIA
　　Yes, husband; now what do you say?

DUKE ORSINO
[To VIOLA] Her husband, sir?

VIOLA
　　My lord, I am not.
I'm afraid this lady's talking rot!

OLIVIA
Do not be afraid to be who you are.
You're denying our love has now gone too far.
Stand proud as my husband and be of good cheer.
You'll be stronger than the man you fear *[Indicating
　　ORSINO]*

　　　　　　[Enter Priest]

O welcome, Father! Now you must share
What happened between me and him *[Indicating VIOLA]*
 in there!

PRIEST
[Indicating VIOLA and OLIVIA] Two hours ago, these two
 and me,
We had a little ceremony.
They exchanged their vows, then I did the business
By pronouncing them wed as Mister and Missus.

DUKE ORSINO
[Indicating VIOLA] You deceitful wretch, such treachery!
All this time you lied to me!
[To OLIVIA] Well take him then; but direct thy feet
To a place where we will never meet.

VIOLA
[Confused] My lord, I beg . . .

OLIVIA
 O, save your breath!
You narrowly escape your death!

[Enter SIR ANDREW]

SIR ANDREW
[Injured] Is there a doctor in the house?
He's broken us, the dirty louse.

OLIVIA
Who's done this? Someone we know.

SIR ANDREW
The count's young man, Cesario.
We thought he would be weak at the knees,
But he fights like bloody Hercules.

DUKE ORSINO
My gentleman, Cesario?

SIR ANDREW
And there he is! You so-and-so!
You cracked my nut.

VIOLA
    You talking to me?
I treated you most decently.

SIR ANDREW
Is that what you call this blood on my head?

[Enter SIR TOBY BELCH and Clown]

If Sir Toby weren't drunk, he'd have hurt you instead!

DUKE ORSINO
Gentleman!

SIR TOBY BELCH
    [Injured and drunk] Do not attack!
I'm hurt enough. Now where's the quack[6]?

Clown
I warn you now, a few he's had.

---

6   Idiom for a doctor who is not good at their job or does not use proper medicine.

SIR TOBY BELCH
A drunk in here? Oh, that's too bad!

OLIVIA
Take him away!

SIR ANDREW
You're in my care.
We'll see the Doctor as a pair.

SIR TOBY BELCH
[Indicating VIOLA] You donkey head! You useless goon!
You monkey bum. You big buffoon.

OLIVIA
Just go and put him in his bed.
And get the doctor to examine his head.

*[Exeunt Clown, FABIAN, SIR TOBY
BELCH, and SIR ANDREW]*

*[Enter SEBASTIAN indicating SIR TOBY and SIR
ANDREW in passing]*

SEBASTIAN
I am sorry if I give offense,
But it was a matter of self-defence.
I would treat my brother equally,
If he had drawn his sword on me.
[To OLIVIA] For the sake of our vows and that ring on
your hand,
Please tell me that you understand!

DUKE ORSINO

[Seeing VIOLA and SEBASTIAN together] One face, one
    voice, one big confusion,

This is a strange and unholy illusion.

SEBASTIAN

My dear Antonio! There you are!

I've been looking for you both near and far.

ANTONIO

Sebastian?

SEBASTIAN

    Yes, the one and the same!

ANTONIO

There's another of you who bears the same name.

OLIVIA

Most wonderful!

SEBASTIAN

    [Seeing VIOLA] What trick is this Mister?

You look like my twin, but she was my sister.

So where are you from? And what does this mean?

VIOLA

I landed here from Messaline.

Sebastian was the man who married my mother,

A nobleman who gave his name to my brother,

Who died in a shipwreck over three months dispatched.

You must be his spirit!

SEBASTIAN
With a body attached?!
If you weren't a man, which would be a surprise,
I would call you Viola and have tears in my eyes.

VIOLA
On my thirteenth birthday, my dad left this earth.

SEBASTIAN
And mine as well. And a mark of his birth
He had above

VIOLA AND SEBASTIAN
[Realizing they are twins] His right eyebrow!

VIOLA
Do not embrace me. Let's wait for now.
My ladies' clothes are held in town.
By an old sea dog. I'll get them sent around.

SEBASTIAN
We'll save our reunion until you are dressed.

VIOLA
[Indicating ORSINO and OLIVIA] My life on this isle
    between these two was blessed

SEBASTIAN
[To OLIVIA] It seems you were indeed deceived.
But you've married a man, so you must be relieved!

DUKE ORSINO
If his blood is noble, then yours must be too.

You told me you loved me. Is that still true?

VIOLA
I stand by everything I said.

DUKE ORSINO
[To VIOLA] Go grab your dress! Let's go get wed.

VIOLA
He's in jail, the captain who looks after my clothes

OLIVIA
Is he? On whose orders?

VIOLA
    Malvolio's

OLIVIA
Bring him right here. I do not want to wait.
The last time I saw him he was in a bit of a state.

[Re-enter Clown with a letter and FABIAN]

Clown
I bring news from Malvolio.
Since he left, he's laying low,
Possessed by devils, such a pity.
I bring from him a little ditty.

OLIVIA
Well don't stand gaping. Read it now

Clown
It's crazy talk. I don't know how./

OLIVIA
Crazy talk's your specialty.

FABIAN
I'll read it. Ma'am. Give it to me.
[Reading] 'I swear to God you've done me wrong.
I was locked in a dungeon for far too long.
Sir Toby said I was wrong in the head,
But I know that I was terribly led.
I have the letter you did send
That nearly sent me around the bend
And with that from this isle I'll go.
Signed, the poor Malvolio'.

OLIVIA
Did he write this?

Clown
    It is from he!

DUKE ORSINO
He doesn't sound insane to me

OLIVIA
Fabian, go and bring him here.

                    [Exit FABIAN]

I'd like to share some thoughts, my dear.
As my future brother-in-law,

Get married here.

DUKE ORSINO
Well, if you are sure!
[To VIOLA] I'm sure I want to marry you
After everything that we've been through.
You've called me Master through all our strife.
Now you will be your master's wife.

VIOLA
My husband.

OLIVIA
My sister!

[Re-enter FABIAN with MALVOLIO]

DUKE ORSINO
And who is this 'guest'?

MALVOLIO
Malvolio, sir, at my madam's request.

OLIVIA
Malvolio? It's been too long.

MALVOLIO
Madam, you have done me wrong.
This is the letter you sent to me

[Hands the fake letter to OLIVIA]

That took away my modesty
That had me grinning, just for starters

And wearing yellow socks and garters!
In turn, it got me locked away
In the dark both night and day.
Sir Toby tried to drive me mad.
Oh what a lot of fun you had.
I will not stand here now and cry,
But maybe you could tell me why!

OLIVIA

[Reading the fake letter]

After studying this a little while,
I can honestly say it's not my style.
It looks like it's Maria's wit,
And now I come to think of it,
It was she who told me you were mad!
Malvolio, we've both been had!
What a terrible girl Maria is!
And I'm sure she had accomplices!
But console yourself and all your fury,
For you will be their judge and jury.

FABIAN

Let's not spoil this wonderful time.
Sir Toby and I were her partners in crime.
Maria wrote the actual letter.
No one could have done it better.
We wanted to throw him under a bus
Because he was always so rude to us
But now let's all let bygones be.

OLIVIA

Malvolio, how they baffled thee!

Clown

[As Topas to Malvolio]

You recognise these tones at least?

I am Sir Topas, your prison's priest.

You said that I was 'low of wit'.

Now you're lower than me, so think on it!

MALVOLIO

I'll get you all back if it's the last thing I do.

[Exit]

OLIVIA

That really was most cruel of you.

DUKE ORSINO

Follow him and calm his fear.

[To VIOLA]

We need to see your captain here.

You look good as a boy, but I have to confess,

I'd like to see you in a dress.

We'll stick around until it arrives.

And then we'll get married and start our new lives.

Me with her *[Referring to VIOLA]*, and *[Referring to SEBASTIAN]* him with you

It's all turned out fine. I knew it would do.

Clown

[Singing to the tune of 'The Wild Rover']

The story is over. Our Twelfth Night is done,
As we wait for the rise of the thirteenth day's sun.
We'll go back to normal with the wind and the rain,
But maybe next year, we'll come shine again.
And its oh nay never,
Make of it 'What you will'.
Until the same time next year, we wish you no ill!

More Drama Resources from Alphabet Publishing

Silly Shakespeare for Students by Paul Leonard Murray

A Midsummer Night's Dream
Macbeth
Pericles
Hamlet
Othello
Twelfth Night

Short Original Plays by Alice Savage

Just Desserts: A foodie drama about a chef gone bad
Introducing Rob: Lola's family loves her new boyfriend. Until they actually meet him
Colorado Ghost Story: Two exchange students get into trouble in the old West
Strange Medicine: Who decides what the truth is?

The Drama Book: Lesson Plans, Activities, and Scripts for the English Language Classroom

ISTD Coursebooks by Alice Savage

Her Own Worst Enemy: A serious comedy about choosing a major
Only the Best Intentions: A love triangle between a guy, a girl and a game
Rising Water: A stormy drama about what happens to people in a crisis

Alphabet Publishing is an independent publisher of creative and innovative educational material. Learn more at www.alphabetpublishingbooks.com.

www.ingramcontent.com/pod-product-compliance
Lightning Source LLC
Chambersburg PA
CBHW021650120626
46545CB00002B/785